FINDING GIFTS
IN DEPRESSION

FINDING GIFTS IN DEPRESSION
AN ARTIST'S JOURNEY

CAROLYN FREEMAN HANSEN

iUniverse, Inc.
New York Lincoln Shanghai

Finding Gifts in Depression
An Artist's Journey

iUniverse books may be ordered through booksellers or by contacting:

iUniverse
2021 Pine Lake Road, Suite 100
Lincoln, NE 68512
www.iuniverse.com
1-800-Authors (1-800-288-4677)

Because of the dynamic nature of the Internet, any Web addresses or links contained in this book may have changed since publication and may no longer be valid.

The information, ideas, and suggestions in this book are not intended as a substitute for professional advice. Before following any suggestions contained in this book, you should consult your personal physician or mental health professional. Neither the author nor the publisher shall be liable or responsible for any loss or damage allegedly arising as a consequence of your use or application of any information or suggestions in this book.

ISBN: 978-0-595-42527-3 (pbk)
ISBN: 978-0-595-86856-8 (ebk)

Printed in the United States of America

Contents

Prelude to Understanding

ο ο ο ο ο ο ο ο ο ο ο ο ο ο ο ο ο ο ο ο ο ο ο ο ο ο ο ο ο ο ο ο ο

Be kind, for everyone you meet is fighting a great battle.
—Philo of Alexandria, 20 BCE–50CE, Hellenized Jew

When others give us presents that make us want to puke, most of us flash a superficial smile and think, "Why would they give this to me? I don't want it, I don't need it, and I don't like it." Or, "She probably bought it at a garage sale. Maybe someone gave it to her and she wanted to get rid of it." Or even, "Does he hate me? Is this a joke?"

Depression is filled with unwanted gifts. I didn't want them and definitely didn't like them; and, for many years, I thought I didn't need them. Like any other gifts I hated, I pushed my depression into a cold basement and tried to forget about it.

But the gifts of depression, unlike rhinestone-encrusted stiletto heels or a Chia Pet, won't stay in the basement. They creep up the stairs in bits and pieces until they completely consume who we are, what we do, and how we treat our friends and family. When we refuse to unwrap these gifts, they growl like a vicious black dog, making us anxious, self-conscious, and terribly sad. They won't leave us alone until we tear off the wrapping and embrace the unwanted contents. But when we do, peace finds us. That's what this book is about.

I'm assuming that, if you're reading this book, you suffer from depression, or you love someone who does. You may be wondering, *How do I unwrap the gifts of depression?*

There is no medical degree on my résumé; I'm not a therapist, psychologist, or psychiatrist. I am an artist who found that my unwanted depression was filled with gifts. By creating art, I examined my inner demons from new perspectives. By unwrapping the gift of nightmares and writing in my journal, I became aware of wonderful and unexpected teachings. I also consulted my physician, counselors, a massage therapist, and an acupuncturist. All these efforts helped me find the courage to unwrap my depression and restore my life. What I found, I give to you.

I hope that my experiences will help you find healing. You are not alone! Be courageous and embrace the gifts of depression.

A Letter from My Husband

Dear Reader,

You are about to join my wife on her roller-coaster ride through clinical depression. I have been on that journey with her. It is a fascinating, frightening, and yet productive trip.

She learned along the way that she did not travel alone. She needed the help of many people. I very much appreciate our family and friends who were encouraging and understood what she was going through.

I also appreciate the help she received from physicians and therapists, including emotional and physical therapists and acupuncturists.

But mostly I appreciate this 120-pound dynamo who calmly sleeps beside me each night. She eventually got the courage to say to the black dog of depression, "You S.O.B., you snarl at me once more, and I'm going to kick your ass!" And he snarled. And she kicked his ass.

Will she someday make another trip through the topsy-turvy world of depression? I don't know. But I do know that, if she does, I'll be with her.

Harlan Hansen

The Gift of Haunting Dreams

Who looks outside, dreams. Who looks inside, awakens.

—Carl Jung

1999

February 1

A sneering doctor chases me around his office with a dripping syringe, an evil glare on his grungy face, and grunting sounds of gratification. Dressed in a vomit-colored smock, he insists on giving me an unneeded and unwanted shot.

February 9

Stinking brown water covers the floor of the bathroom. The stool erupts, dumping more of the smelly mess. I try to escape but the stairway is gone. Hanging from the ceiling is an old rope and I swing to a filthy lab floor. Suddenly in my hand is a sculpture of a distorted gargoyle.

A robot moves toward me. He grabs the sculpture and stares at me through beady eyes, laughs maliciously and disappears.

Piercing eyes stare through a dark mist. An eerie sound surrounds me. I stumble as I try to hide. A growling black dog steps out of the darkness. He bares his fangs as he grows larger. His head moves closer with an evil sneer.

February 11

What are my chaotic dreams telling me? They go on night after night. Last night they were filled with rebellious, lime green naked people with distorted bodies. They danced around me and jumped in my face, emitting their skunk breath. Hollering, their bodies began to melt.

After months of my nightmares becoming more and more gruesome, I could no longer deny something was seriously wrong—but what?

Over the years, something unseen had been taking over my emotions, but I wouldn't acknowledge it. As long as I could get my children through the day, escape to my studio, and keep constantly busy, I could pretend nothing was destroying me.

My husband and I had ways of getting me over the humps. When we visited relatives for the holidays, we took a motel room, so I could be alone and cry. Sometimes I would shake uncontrollably, and Harlan would take my hands, look me in the eyes, and we would breathe deeply and slowly. I foolishly believed no one knew anything was wrong.

I thought if I could just get rid of these horrible nightmares, I could pull myself together. The longer I stuck my head in the mud and yelled "I'm not listening!" to my subconscious, the louder my subconscious became.

Then came the most haunting dream of all:

A strange silence and a mysterious mist appeared. Suddenly there was an egg with a spiral behind it, and written on each were fractal geometric formulas. Gasping for breath, I stared at it.

I awoke stunned. With eyes wide open, I realized I could no longer pretend everything was all right.

I picked this dream apart. What did the icons mean? Why an egg? An egg is a seed, a new beginning, unexplored territory, an entrance to an unknown world, and an extremely private place. The egg told me I was entering an uncharted existence.

Spirals go up and down, showing as much as they hide. They have the light side and the dark side, the known and the unknown. Was the spiral telling me I would learn, descend, recharge, and move upward, repeating the process many times?

Finally, there were the geometric formulas. Fractal geometric formulas depict repeating irregular curves or shapes. I had seen a fascinating television program on PBS called *Colors of Infinity* about fractal geometric formulas and the ingenuity of nature. These formulas reinforced what the spiral had told me.

All of the icons supported one another, but I wanted to know more. I put down my journal and headed for my studio. The best way to explore this dream's meaning was through art. I needed to immerse my body and mind in these symbols. I unwrapped the dream with days of drawing, painting, and incising mat board, and I discovered both beautiful art and insight.

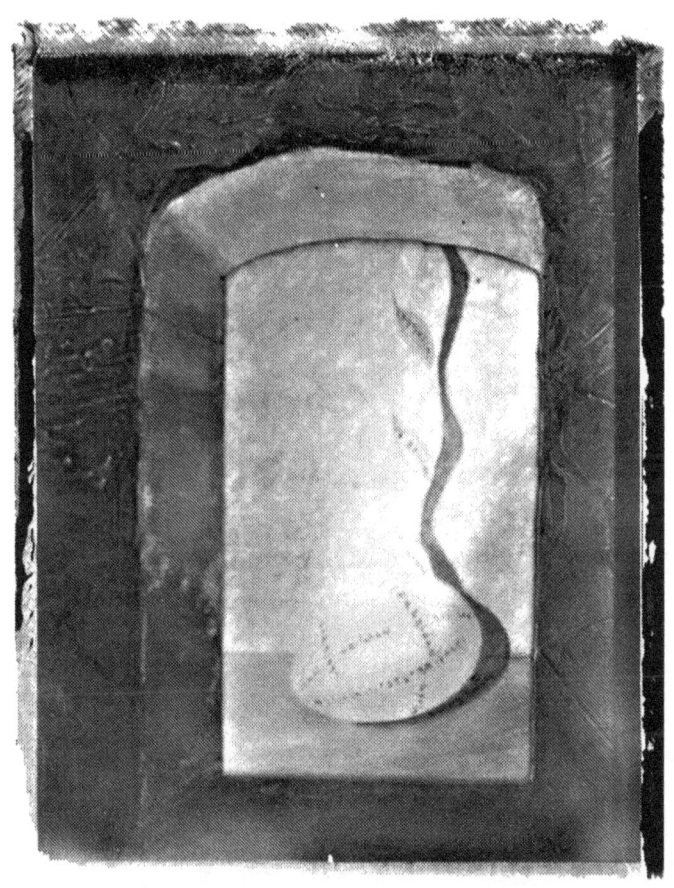

The Egg and I

Transition had entered my life. I was moving toward the unknown. I realized I hadn't been listening to what my crying and trembling spells were trying to tell me, so my dreams had taken over the job. My unhappiness wasn't a product of my children or husband. I wasn't merely stressed from keeping busy. I had the disease of depression. The journey of healing would be long, frightening, and arduous. And it had just begun.

Friend to Friend

Nightmares had long been a part of my life, but it was only when depression arrived that I realized they were a gift. You can either ignore them, or watch in horror as they worsen. But when you unwrap them, you find ways to heal.

As you record your dreams, they may not make any sense in the beginning. However, as time goes on, you will start to see a pattern, and your "dream muscle" will provide you with more and more information. Your nightmares provide insight; don't waste them.

Creative Healing

Creativity is in everyone—in the clothes we wear, in the cars we drive, in the meals we prepare. Find your passion, and follow it.

These creative ideas are designed to help you explore images. Try using these ideas to unwrap the gift of your dreams. Doing something creative, no matter what it is, may give you a clearer perspective.

• Read Eric Maisel's book, *Sleep Thinking*, to discover how you can use your sleep time to resolve problems. Follow his suggestions, such as falling asleep with wonder about your dreams, surrendering to nighttime dream work, and accepting that you need to make changes.

• Buy a special journal in which to record and analyze your dreams and thoughts. Keep it beside your bed or wherever you will use it. When your nocturnal visions awaken you, immediately record them.

• Use multicolored markers or crayons to create abstracted images, drawings, or collages that express the feelings in your nightmares.

Helpful Resources

These resources may help you investigate your dreams. Don't let anyone interpret your dreams. You are the only one who knows what they mean. However, groups that explore the dream world can be helpful.

Books:

Inner Work by Robert A. Johnson

Sleep Thinking by Eric Maisel

A Little Course in Dreams by Robert Bosnak

The Power of your Subconscious Mind by Dr. Joseph Murphy

Memories, Dreams, Reflections by C. G. Jung

Web sites:

lucidity.com/NL11.DreamRecall.html

rider.edu/suler/dreams.html

crystalinks.com/fractal.html

ericmaisel.com

The Gift of Creating

○ ○

Carolyn's work is beautiful, but it always has a dark side.

—A patron's comment about my art

1949

March 13

Today I am twelve. It is nearly spring, but inside me nothing grows. The drizzle from the gray Nebraska sky mirrors my tears as water drips down the screens of my chicken-coop playhouse.

I huddle in a corner trying to avoid the creeping onslaught of imaginary, clammy fingers.

Why are my parents destroying our family? They quarrel every night, and their fights become more and more malicious. Liquor bottles, beer cans, and cigarette butts fill our home. At night, I bury myself under pillows and blankets, hoping to silence their screams.

March 20

My mother enters my bedroom trying to kiss me goodnight. The smell of beer and tobacco are her perfume. I turn away, pretending to be asleep.

Mom told me she didn't want children. She was sure my dad had poked a hole in the condoms.

Fifty years later
1999

February 18

I am exhausted. I can't get everything done.

Screaming, I slump forward and grab my stomach, pleading for help. My husband rushes into my studio and tries to chase away the demons that surrounded me.

The poor guy. He stares at me with wide eyes. Sobbing, I dump my pile of rotten fish on him; he does not interrupt me.

He does not tell me I have entered a brackish abyss filled with decaying, underwater monsters. He wants to help, but neither of us knows what he can do.

His face is covered with worry, and there are tears in his eyes; he insists I call my doctor. My doctor says my serotonin level has dropped, and she suggests I go on medication and see a counselor.

Drugs—are you kidding? Not me!

But, I did agree to see the therapist. Frightening memories quickly came to the surface. Both of my parents were alcoholics. Our childhood, my brother's and mine, was filled with chaos. There were many nights when we would awaken to hear our parents fighting; we would beg them to stop. I can still hear the shattering of glass as my father broke into our home. I still see him attacking my mother with a broken beer bottle, and I still hear my brother screaming at my father not to hurt my mother.

In the summers of these tumultuous years, I would crawl up into an old cottonwood that overhung the roof of my playhouse or hide in a nearby, weeping willow tree house. No one knew I was there, and I could watch the clouds, dream, write in my journal, and cry. Hiding was the best way I could think of to celebrate my twelfth birthday. It was the best way to spend every day. I was trying to hide my life.

I realized, sitting in my therapist's office, that when I was young, I tried to ignore my parents and conceal my life. When that didn't stop the pain, I crept deeper into hiding, until I didn't know who I was.

Despair, like the hungry, vicious, black dog of my dreams, attacked me, and I fled to my studio. There, among my jumble of art supplies and papers, I found a poem I'd written years ago and titled "Hidden." Copies were in my sketchbook, wedged in my journal and in my quotation collection. This gift had been trying to tell me over and over that hiding from myself was not the answer. I read the poem with fresh eyes and began crying at what it told me: Carolyn, you are an artist, and it's time to come out of hiding.

Hidden
beneath layers of facade
behind years of restraint
AND BURIED
in years of conformity
of trying to please
of wanting acceptance
THERE LIES
a voice of purity
and love
SEEKING
only freedom
to be
unique and true.

Who was I as an artist? I needed to accept my artistic gift. Why did I have to become depressed to see what was part of me?

I decided "Hidden" needed to be an assemblage. Assemblage is three-dimensional piece of art created from meaningful objects.

A decade ago part of me knew I was in trouble. For too long, I had lived under a destructive façade. I had to accept who I was. I needed to be me. I needed to come out of hiding.

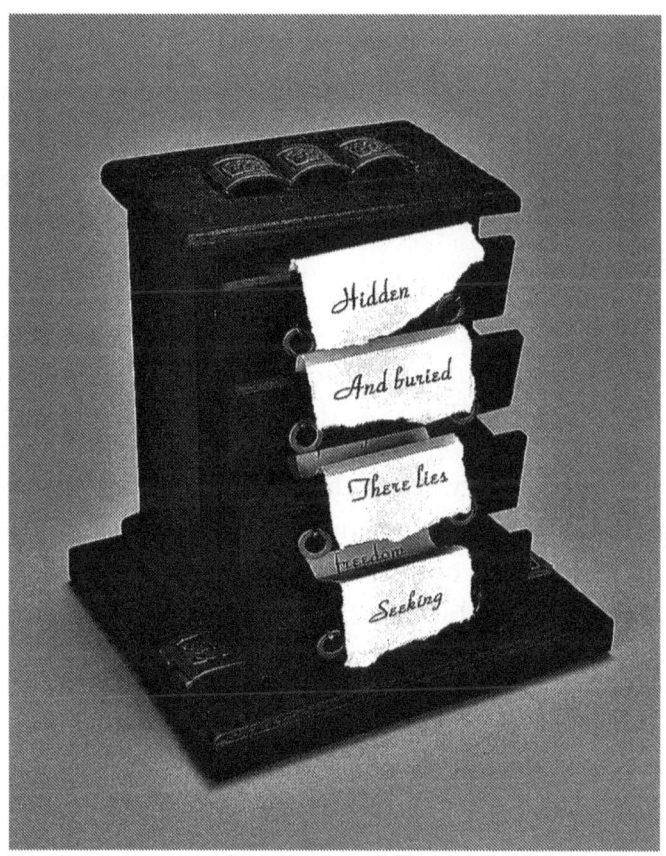

Hidden

While bringing my childhood out of hiding proved a messy form of relief, bringing my artistic side out of hiding was easier and less painful. My next step was to venture beyond the safety of my studio. I wanted to attend a workshop on creating assemblages, but I had never found one. Then, my annual copy of the Anderson Ranch Art Center class schedule arrived. One of the well-known instructors was William Christenberry. He's an East Coast artist with an incredible passion for creating three-dimensional images from photos he has taken of his beloved South. Excitement filled my being, and I signed up for his class.

Anderson Ranch is located near Aspen, Colorado, in the village of Snowmass, and is surrounded by the natural beauty of mountains, streams, trees, and vibrant blue skies. In this realm of natural artistic splendor, the extraordinary Christenberry taught me to believe in my work and in myself.

The atmosphere at Anderson Ranch was so pure that I feasted on it like a chocoholic consuming delicious fudge. The air I breathed filled me with energy and opened doors to my imagination.

The first day of class we went to the Aspen landfill, a euphemism for the dump, and not my usual stomping grounds. We were looking for treasures to use in the creation of art. The Aspen landfill is well ordered, almost surreal, but Aspen is not your run-of-the-mill town!

In the center of the landfill were two burned-out cars that had careened down a mountainside. In both automobiles, the glass was charred and broken. Chunks of the windshields were sprawled across the scorched hoods.

My heart ached for those whose lives had ended and for the suffering of loved ones left behind. My first thought was that I should not take pieces of the windshields because they were embedded with grief.

But something told me I must. On the ground near the cars lay a rusted piece of old wire and a discarded film reel. I picked them up and hauled these symbols of broken memories back to the studio.

As I worked with the pieces and absorbed their energy, I found I had something in common with these charred, broken bits of glass. My soul felt burned out and shattered, broken and abandoned. Like the cars carrying their hapless passengers, my violent childhood had sent me careening and crashing. With these materials, I discovered a way to bring my past out of hiding and into my art. The assemblage, "Without Consent" created itself.

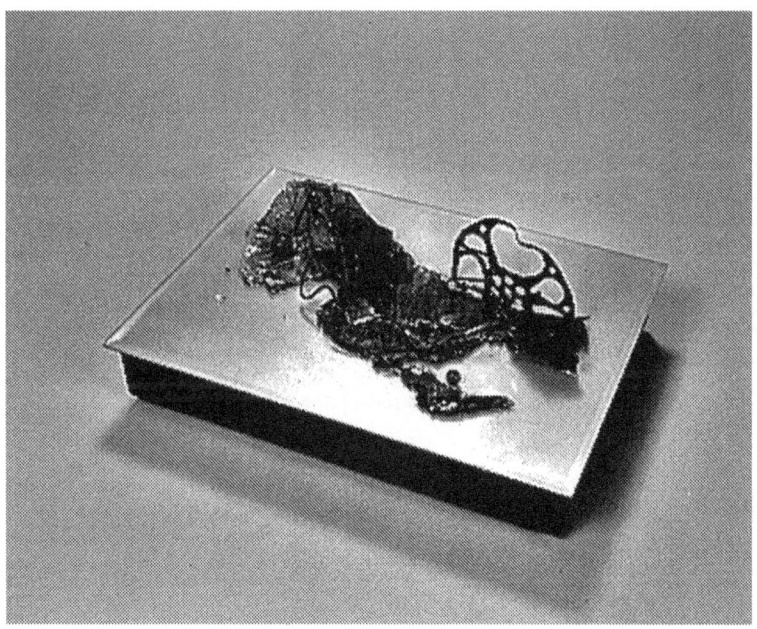

Without Consent

The broken glass forms a horizontal wall of destruction. The rusted film reel portrays the fragility of life. The wire is a metaphor for the undulation of the road we travel. No one asked these people if they wanted their lives to change. No options were given.

I now realized the marvelous gift my art was giving me. Creating art gave me a sense of identity, and that, in turn, gave me courage to confront my painful memories. Finally, I could confront them. Finally, I could come out of hiding.

Friend to Friend

Do we conceal our pain because it's less frightening than going through the grueling tasks of change? The problem with hiding your pain is that it only becomes worse as it festers and rots inside you. You may know the symptoms all too well—nightmares, the need to flee from friends and family, feeling right on the edge of losing control, terrible sadness. Some people take their lives—the ultimate hiding—when their pain has become too much to handle. Are you hiding from your pain?

The way to stop hiding is to make it less painful, and I know of no better way than through creativity. Any sort of creative outlet can make coming out from under your blanket easier. Creativity allows you to pour the pain into words or clay or photos or gardening or whatever exposes your creativity and allows you to heal.

Oftentimes, the media you choose, just like the broken windshield and old film reel I chose, can offer insight into your buried wounds.

Creative Healing

Try some of these ideas to bring yourself out of hiding:

• Take photographs of people, objects and nature that touch you. Have several sizes of your prints made or print them yourself. Turn them over so you cannot see the images. Boldly cut them into a variety of shapes and sizes. Mix all the pieces up and then start turning them over.

Listening only to your inner voice, create a collage. When doing this by hand, I use a nonpermanent adhesive so I can move the photos around, or I scan them and create images on the computer. I also add words or icons when I feel I need them. Put the collages where you will see them every day. From viewing them, you will learn things about yourself you had not been aware existed.

• Create a meal with your friends using recipes you have never tried before. Use edible flowers to adorn the plates, fresh herbs in the entrée, and exotic fruits and cheeses for dessert. Enjoy creating new things even though some are not what you hoped they would be.

• Write "From What Am I Hiding?" in your journal and explore where the words take you. Examine your thoughts and mull them over until you decide they are not going to control you.

• Make cards that say "Do it now," "I like me," "I control my life," "I do my best," or whatever affirmations will help you become a stronger person. Put them in plain sight where you will see them often. Believe what they say. If the cards get shabby, make new ones. You must believe in yourself.

Helpful Resources

Books:

Fearless Creating by Eric Maisel

The Artist's Way by Julia Cameron

Finding Your Own North Star by Martha Beck

12 Secrets of Highly Creative Women by Gail McMeekin

Web sites:

ericmaisel.com

theartistsway.com

marthabeck.com

creativesuccess.com

snowmass.org/index.htm

andersonranch.org

Accepting the Gift of Help

o o o o o o o o o o o o o o o o o o o o o o o o o o o o o o o o

We must be willing to get rid of the life we've planned, so as to have the life that is waiting for us.

—Joseph Campbell

1994

September 10

I was sitting at my desk when one of my friends called. We chatted for a minute and she asked me if I was okay.

Of course, I said. What a strange question. "No, you're not," she said. "Something is terribly wrong." I continued to deny there was anything askew, and we said good-bye.

Within a few minutes, my husband called. My friend had phoned him, saying I was in trouble. All of a sudden, I began to cry. My mask was gone. I had nothing left to hide behind.

September 14

Yesterday my friend and I had an honest chat. She told me about a colleague who is a psychologist and offers counseling by telephone.

Today I had my first session with him. One of the things he told me was, when you are married to a charismatic individual, your life can be difficult.

For me, that is true. I have tried to be like my husband, but I am not. He enjoys big groups of people frequently. I want small groups of friends occasionally. He likes talking in front of a crowd. I avoid public speaking. He delegates with charisma. I do everything myself.

Five years later
1999

September 21

My father's suicide scarred the living, especially my family, yet I have decided to end my life. I will write letters, send them to those who are caring figures in my life, and tell them there was nothing they could have done.

Finding a motel, mailing the letters, and taking a lethal amount of sleeping pills will end my pain.

By the time they get the letters, I will no longer have to struggle against a vicious current.

Ironic, isn't it? I will take drugs to end my life but not to save it.

Coming out of hiding was easier when it meant getting lost in creating art; but it was more difficult when it meant admitting to my friends and family that I couldn't hold it all together. And, while I was doing a little better talking with the therapist, the black dog of depression remained hot on my trail. I had even given him a name: Brainturd. This horrible dog growled at me. With dripping teeth, he chased my thoughts. I tried to turn to art for help, but I had no direction. Despair crept over me, and I just wanted my life to end.

At my husband's prodding, I again talked with my doctor. I lied when she asked me if I had been contemplating suicide but reluctantly agreed to try the medication.

It was weeks before the medication began to change the way I looked at things, but I knew that, if I were going to save my life, I had to put aside my pride and quit trying to beat depression all by myself. Thus, depression gave me another needed gift—the ability to accept help.

When I told my therapist about my new willingness to let others help me, he applauded my growth. He suggested I see a psychiatric nurse who was also an acupuncturist. I had been to an acupuncturist years ago and had not found the treatment helpful. However, trusting my analyst and knowing he understood my journey, I made an appointment for counseling and acupuncture.

From the first therapy session, I told the acupuncturist things I did not tell my male therapist. I had never given it any thought before, but I discovered that male and female energies are different. After our talk, the acupuncturist instructed me to lie down while she inserted hair-thin needles into pressure points in my hands, arms, and legs. Then she left.

At first, I didn't like being in that room alone with all those needles sticking out of me. My acupuncturist wouldn't even let her dog stay in the same room with me. She told me I had so much negative energy that she did not want her pet to absorb it.

I was supposed to lie still. It was like trying to stop a sneeze. A stream of images emerged that I did not understand. I left exhausted. The acupuncturist warned me that frightening emotions, depressing thoughts, and terrifying scenes would continue to present themselves without warning.

I cried a lot the next day, but she had told me to expect that reaction. I had dumped a lot of garbage, especially anger. I don't know how quickly I might have measured the depth of my anger with only counseling. Acupuncture accelerated my healing and revealed issues I was not aware of. The painful side about getting rid of all this muck was that I mourned. These emotions had been a part of my life for so long that I missed them.

My acupuncturist recommended I see a massage therapist who was attuned to the energy within our bodies. What an incredible gift to find these two women! As a result of the sessions with the acupuncturist and the massage therapist, my body started to relax and regenerate, and my nightmares dwindled. The backyard of my soul became a garden of budding plants. No longer did I feel the need to kill myself.

About this time, I recorded a wonderful dream in my journal.

1999

October 13

My grandma appears in a doorway and says, "I have come to help." I faint.

I need help, and of all the people I have known, my grandma will help me and not send a bill.

Unwrapping the gift of acceptance, I received the help I never thought I needed from my family, my friends, medication, counseling, acupuncture, and massage. And that sparked the idea for another assemblage.

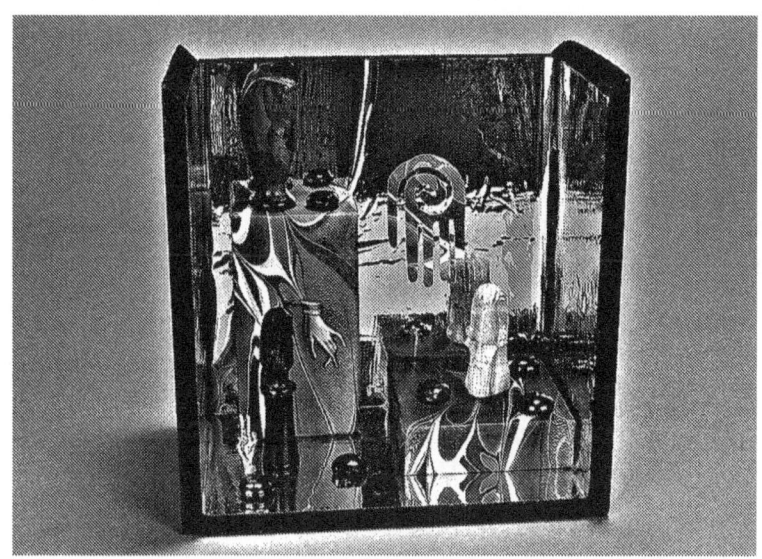

The Handless Maiden

A person with no hands must accept help from others. In doing so, she does not admit weakness, but instead becomes a powerful woman with countless hands.

Friend to Friend

Just as I was wrapping up this chapter, I received word that a dear friend of mine had committed suicide. She was only fifty-three. At her memorial service, attended by more than four hundred people, a man said, "She had a great sorrow within her that she could not share and could not live with." None of us had any idea of her suffering. Yet, if she had shared it with us, she might still be alive.

I can understand why she wanted to hide her pain. There are times when we feel the things we have done are unforgivable, and admitting one's inner pain is often considered a weakness. We were raised in a generation that did not discuss such things as depression and anxiety, except to refer to those folks as "crazy people."

My hurting friend, you are not crazy; you are ill. Just as you cannot cure cancer on your own, you cannot cure your depression by yourself. It's not a weakness to be sick. But it is a weakness to think you can magically overcome depression without help.

Admitting you cannot beat your depression alone is a great strength. Unwrap the powerful gift of acceptance. Don't be afraid to seek out help from family, friends, medication, counseling, and alternative therapies.

If you decide to try acupuncture, recommendations from your doctor or therapist may guide you in finding someone who will help you. Always inform your healthcare providers about any treatment you are considering.

Acupuncture originated over two thousand years ago in China. Acupuncture needles are metallic, solid, and hair-thin. Most of us feel little or no discomfort. The U.S. Food and Drug Administration (FDA) has approved acupuncture needles for use by licensed practitioners since 1996. The FDA requires that needles be sterile, nontoxic, and labeled for single use by qualified practitioners.

Whether or not you try acupuncture, do try massage therapy. If I could give each of you one gift, it would be what my massage therapist gives to me. Her magic fingers release my muscle tension and make me feel whole again. So, from my heart, I send you this wonder, and I wish you the courage to embrace it.

Creative Healing

These suggestions may encourage you to accept help from others:

• With a close friend, go to garage sales, junk stores, and secondhand shops. Find the most outrageous thing you can dress up in: a funny hat, a multicolored boa, outrageous sunglasses, a wild pair of boots, or whatever strikes you as hilarious. Laughing is one of the most healing things you can do.

• Invite a friend to help you with a home improvement project, such as painting a room, tiling a bathroom, or landscaping your garden. Have carry-out for lunch, relax and enjoy.

Helpful Resources

Books:

Angry Housewives Eating Bon Bons by Lorna Landvik

The Kite Runner by Khaled Hosseini

The Glass Castle: A Memoir by Jeannette Walls

The Persian Pickle Club by Sandra Dallas

Movies:

An Intimate Friendship

Fried Green Tomatoes

Beaches

An Officer and a Gentleman

Web sites:

nimh.nih.gov/publicat/depression.cfm

nccam.nih.gov/health/acupuncture/

101lifestyle.com/beauty/massage/massage.html

The Gift of Forgiveness

○ ○

Forgiveness does not change the past, but it does enhance the present.

—Carolyn Hansen

1952

May 8

Mom has been telling me Dad is sleeping with another woman, and he is doing it to hurt her. This other woman is ugly and stupid.

I have ignored my mom's drunken ravings. But today, as I cut through the back room of my father's drug store, I saw a woman on a ladder with my dad's hand up her dress.

I will never forget the look on my father's face. He has not only hurt Mom, he has destroyed any relationship we had.

Forty-seven years later
1999

August 3

My depression has returned, and my husband is angry. He feels I use depression as a facade so I don't have to confront issues. He doesn't want to endure my torment again; it has been painful enough. He does not want any more stress in his life. He tells me to fix it by saying, "You did it before, you can do it again."

I didn't think the black dog would return. But he did. He growled and snarled at me, digging up all the newly planted flowers in my soul. I screamed at him, "I don't like you!" But Brainturd didn't care. He just stared at me with his bloodshot eyes and kept digging. I felt like an overripe banana with diseased, rotten skin. The words, *it would be easier to let the dog get me*, flashed across my mind, and I knew I was in trouble.

When I had issues I didn't want to address, depression was one of my escape mechanisms—my husband was right. I would sleep more and retreat into a darkened world in a vain attempt to numb the pain, but my sleep would be fitful and filled with nightmares. Up to this point, my husband had been kind and supporting; yet, strangely, my husband's anger was what I needed this time. I am stubborn, and when someone refuses to help me, I decide I'll do it by myself—the little red hen syndrome.

More counseling sessions, acupuncture therapy, and massages. More negative memories surfaced. My pathway out of this depressive episode became clear: I needed to unwrap the gift of forgiveness. As much as I did not want to, I needed to let go of my anger at people who hurt me, starting with my parents.

I was angry with my father. I couldn't forgive him for his drunken stupors, the times he gambled and drank in the basement with his friends while Mom was at market, or when he attacked Mom in a drunken rage. My anger was so great that, when he died in 1962, I didn't even go to his funeral.

It was no better with my mother. I was still angry for her unkind words when I was a child, for making me feel stupid, for the smell of beer and cigarettes that surrounded her, for my not being able to have friends in our home, and for driving Dad to another woman. Dad had committed suicide, but Mom wanted it to be murder so she could collect the insurance money.

The journey of forgiving my father and mother required I put on hip-waders and march through the muck of my past. Memories years old seemed as fresh and painful as if they were in the present. They controlled my thoughts as I traveled back in time. I felt like a tragic time traveler.

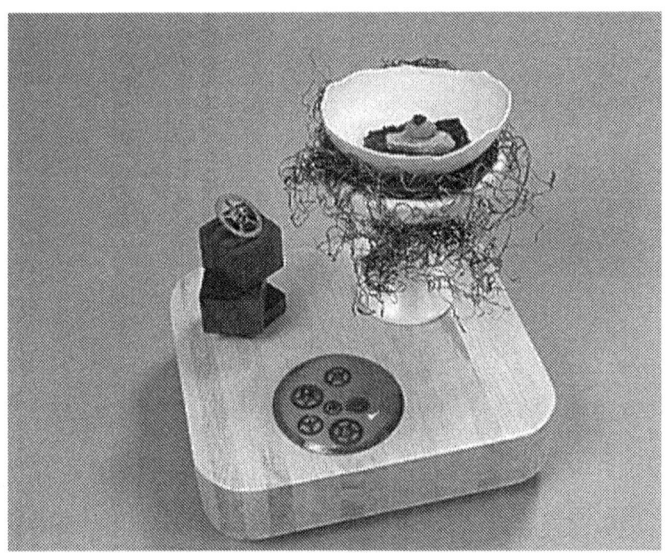

Time Travel

Although a journey back in time is sometimes necessary for a wound to heal, we must always journey back to the present telling ourselves, What's done is done. We cannot change the past, but we can forgive and find peace.

The shattered nest was a symbol of my confused life. The blocks expressed the fragility of life, and the timepieces represented the fact that time does not stand still. The pile of stones within the eggshell was a signpost directing me which way to go.

The assemblage allowed me to explore anger and bitterness with my hands, as well as with my mind and heart. I came to understand my mother and father were human beings who endured psychological pain—just as I was doing. They chose alcohol, violence, and destructive words to deal with their pain, but they had not been out to hurt me. My parents and I chose different paths, but we were not that different. The raging flame within me melted my anger into a little puddle of wax.

2000

March 23

In my dream, my home burns to the ground, crumbles into ashes, and vanishes.

Suddenly, I'm showering in a tent made of lightweight cloth as my father stands outside to protect me. Nearby is a green pickup, and then an aqua-colored sea of love surrounds me.

I walk into water that is warm and soothing, filling me with peace. In the distance is a group of people who are laughing, dancing, and singing. Joining them, I begin to dance.

I had unwrapped the gift of forgiving my parents. By now, I thought Brainturd would leave me alone. And, for a while, he did. But soon he was back, barking in a frightening frenzy. I needed to forgive myself.

I was always beating up on myself for behaving like an idiot. I can't tell you the number of times I've messed up: forgetting to do things or doing them twice, losing notes I needed and never finding them, driving past the place I want to go because I am in Never-Never Land, putting the mail with the dirty clothes, stewing because I wasn't invited to a party and then realizing I actually had been invited. Even worse, I was angry with myself for saying unkind things about those I did not like and for wanting to get even with others.

If art could help me forgive my mom and dad, could it help me forgive myself? Maybe. I decided to explore this idea, and soon another assemblage evolved.

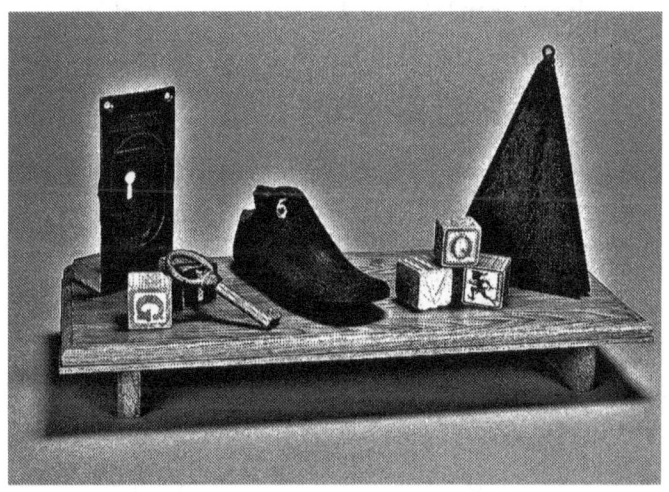

Never-Never Land

Either I do these idiotic things because I am not living in the moment or I make bad decisions. Probably both. My mind is busy processing other "important" information. I am learning that when I throw my glasses in the wastebasket, it is time to slow down and focus on one thing at a time.

The creation of "Never-Never Land" gave me two bits of insight. First, it reminded me that all humans screw up. It is part of the learning process. I needed to forgive myself for not being perfect and for expecting that I should have been.

Second, I learned that I get absent-minded when my brain is busier than it has to be. Without conscious awareness, I drag around sacks of emotional garbage, and my inner trash compactor can't handle the entire mass at once. Instead of getting angry with myself about it, I need to slow down and take out the trash.

I am still learning to deal with hurtful things in my past—both what I and others have done. There are times when agonizing incidents present themselves, and I know I must examine them and then let those destructive moments dissolve into the ether.

I am also learning to focus on the positive sides of "yesterdays." There are pleasant events to remember, memories that make me smile and photos that touched my heart. These images allow me to revisit times of delight, wonder, and happiness.

Friend to Friend

I've heard it said, "Depression is anger turned inward." When anger is turned inside out, depression has nowhere to go but out the window. Do you have anger at people in your past? At your parents? Maybe it's your spouse, your ex, your kids, or—the worst—yourself.

Anger destroys you, while forgiving brings you peace. Most of us do not live in the moment. We dwell in the yesterdays and tomorrows. Living in the past and the future can build overwhelming stress, causing our blood pressure to reach new highs.

If you're angry with someone, consider this: your anger is hurting only you. Forgiveness will make the pain stop. Seek any help you need for learning to forgive, such as counseling, massage, acupuncture, or creativity.

If you're angry with yourself, realize that everyone has regrets. We all remember irrational mumblings or getting angry over a remark that meant no harm. How about the phone calls we didn't make or the appointments we forgot to keep? Or the lies we told because we were afraid to tell the truth?

Too bad life doesn't have a delete key. Or is forgiving the delete key?

Creative Healing

Try some of these ideas to explore letting go of your anger and regrets:

• Buy several sketchbooks and multicolored markers. Place them in your car, at your desk, and any place you spend a lot of time. When you have an angry thought or regret, scribble the emotion in your sketchbook. When you are ready to let go of this emotion, wad up the paper and throw it in the dumpster.

• Travel back in time. Recall your favorite memories. Talk to those who made it special. Realize you added to those wonderful times.

• Find an old photo, watch, catalog, or calendar and start a shrine to the past. When thoughts of yesterdays enter your mind, draw your feelings and include them.

Then build a shrine to today. Add things that are happening in the present, such as a drawing from your child, a hat or scarf you love to wear, a book you find exciting. Remember, the past is gone and tomorrow never comes. Enjoy today.

Helpful Resources

Books:

I Can Do It by Louise L. Hay

Art of Forgiving by Lewis B. Smedes

You Can Heal Your Life by Louise L. Hay

Running On Empty by Ellen Sue Stern

Movie:

The Upside of Anger

Web site:

learningplaceonline.com/spirit/forgive/yourself-others.htm

findinggiftsindepression.com (my art and book)

The Gift of Spirituality

How quick we are to disapprove of what we deem different or impractical.

—Gertrude Mueller Nelson

1998

March 31

In my nocturnal episode, a spiritual being helps me. She is dressed in a long robe that moves in the breeze. Her eyes are soul-searching green. Her skin is clear and smooth as a fragile flower.

But she is not fragile. She watches over me, and like a warm blanket on a cold night, she gives me comfort.

Was the spiritual being in my dream Sophia, the archetypal goddess of wisdom?

I left the church; I left Christianity.

I could hardly believe it! If anyone had told me this was going to happen, I would have thought his or her brain was mush. The church was my security blanket. Every time we moved, one of the first things I looked for was a place to worship. If I did not take communion once a week, I lost what little bearing I had.

One Sunday, however, as I sat in a pew, tears started to roll down my face. After pulling myself together and taking Communion, I quickly left the church. Getting into my car, I had trouble breathing; I was not able to think clearly.

The next Sunday, as I listened to the homily, tears again washed down my cheeks. I left in the middle of the service and rushed to my car, sobbing. When I walked into our home, my husband stared at me in disbelief and asked, "What's wrong?"

I didn't know.

The following week, my husband went to church with me. Halfway through the service, my lip quivering, I tugged on his sleeve, and we left. His arm steadied me. I did not understand what was happening.

The following Sunday, I was scheduled to help with the Eucharist. As I put on my robe, I had an overwhelming sense that this was not something I should do. Hysterical, I told the priest I could no longer help with the Eucharist. Dazed, I stumbled from the church and sat in my car shaking. For some reason, Brainturd sat at the church entrance and growled with glowing eyes. I knew I couldn't go back. My tears signified the loss of what had always been a major part of my life.

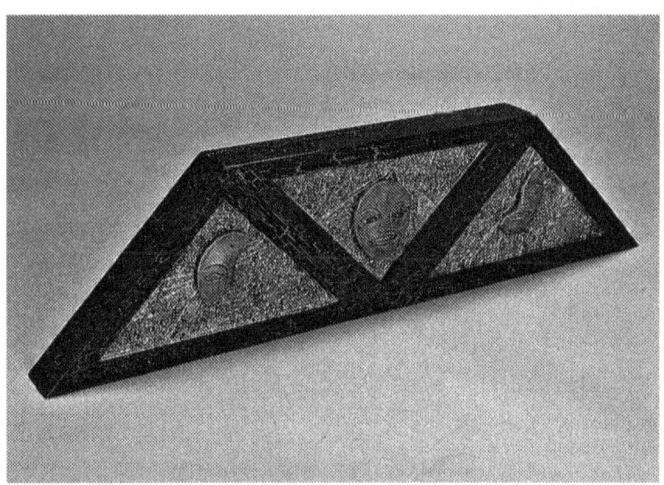

Shattered Dreams

My need for organized religion no longer exists. Why?

I created "Shattered Dreams" with a hammer and elbow grease. Relishing each strike I made on the glass helped me release my anxiety. When the piece was finished, I was ready to explore what was happening to me.

As our oldest son and I were wandering through his backyard, we talked about the change.

"I am not a Christian or a Jew; I'm not Buddhist, Muslim, Hindu, or an atheist—or even an agnostic," I said. "What am I?"

He answered, "Mom, you're a Jedi."

I had spent a lot of time fighting the dark side; I could live with being a Jedi! It was the first step in unwrapping the gift of my own spirituality.

The God presented in church had become too small for me. I could not accept a God who punished and judged. I opened myself to new forms of spirituality, and my concept of God expanded to a Creative Force. The Force now manifests itself to me in many archetypes.

Carl Jung gave meaning to the word "archetype." An archetype is a psychological symbol that comes forth when we need a better understanding of the path we have taken. The symbol often appears as a personality. Jung said there are four main archetypes: the self, the shadow, the anima, and the animus.

My spirit guide, Charlie, is an anima. The Creative Force manifested as Charlie and came when I needed someone I could chew gum with, spit, swear, and scratch my butt—someone who wore faded jeans with holes in them.

One day, on my way to have my hair cut, I felt tears in my eyes. My plea to Charlie was, "Please give me a sign that I am getting better. I need to know I'm improving."

I was in the beauty salon, having my hair shampooed, surrounded by very proper women, and I had this thought: "I could masturbate under this cape and no one would know." What a sign! Not what I had expected, but it made me smile—and it is difficult to be depressed when you smile.

The goddess of wisdom, Sophia, is another anima. She appears in my dreams as a beautiful woman in a flowing gown, with eyes that look straight through to my soul. She teaches me to trust my inner wisdom. When I have a hunch I should or should not do something—like not helping with the Eucharist—I need to pay attention. Charlie wears holey jeans, and Sophia balances me with a sense of the ethereal.

My animas appear as beings outside myself, while the archetype of the shadow manifests itself within me. According to Robert A.

Johnson's book, *Owning Your Own Shadow*, the shadow is the mysterious part of the unconscious. The archetype shadow is not evil; it is, like all of our archetypes, a teacher. We perceive it as evil because it is surrounded by mystery, and we are afraid of it. The shadow is our hidden self, carrying those personality traits society does not accept. Following our own path is not what our material world wants from us.

In the world I was raised, you needed to be a Christian to be accepted. The day I realized I was no longer a Christian was the day my shadow began my liberation.

My most important archetype is, of course, Brainturd. The black dog archetype, often seen as a large hound with glowing red eyes, has appeared to many people with depression—Winston Churchill being one of the most famous. I began to question why my depression manifested itself as a dog. I came up with three answers.

First, dogs bark a warning when something isn't right. Looking back over the years, I noticed Brainturd barked not to harm me, but to warn me. He barked me away from church to protect me from a path I couldn't walk anymore. He barked whenever I was about to career over the edge into depression.

Second, dogs are hunters. Brainturd hunted down what was destroying me and attacked it viciously until I sought healing.

Third, dogs are symbols of trust and loyalty. Now Brainturd lies beside me and is a close friend. He puts his head on my lap when I am going through difficult times.

Brainturd is a gift. He helped me find my way out of depression, and he taught me to be myself. I now call him Brainy.

Depression handed me the gift of my own spirituality. It's a gift I will continue to unwrap for the rest of my life.

Friend to Friend

I have always had an ongoing relationship with God, or the Creative Force, or whatever name we assign this unknown power. I don't know if this entity is male or female, young or old, organic or inorganic, seen or unseen, here or there. I do know that believing in an incredible Creative Being always helps pull my world back together.

Many people suffering from depression find their spirituality (or lack of it) only contributes to their pain. You are a spiritual being created by an infinite, omniscient Force. Exploring your own spirituality is, therefore, a journey too large to fit into any one religion. So, don't be afraid. Unwrap the gift of your spirituality, and embrace the things that make sense for you.

Creative Healing

Try some of these ideas to expand your experience of the Creative Force:

• When archetypes appear in your dreams, nightmares, or visions, know that they are there to teach. They may take the form of doctors, black dogs, fisherwomen, or any number of things. Talk with them, but don't be afraid of them.

Why do you think these archetypes appear? Choose an archetype that has a strong pull on you and write, draw, paint, or sculpt the emotions you associate with it. Are there hidden elements surrounding this archetype? Write any words that come to you; they may not make sense, but they will open doors to unfelt feelings.

• Attend religious services radically different from what you are used to. For example, if you are a Roman Catholic, try a Baptist, a Pentecostal, and a Jewish service. You can find a list of religious organizations in the phone book's yellow pages. Stay open-minded, remembering we all see the world differently. How are these services different? How are they similar? How do the unfamiliar rituals expand your concept of the Creative Force?

Helpful Resources

Books:

The Emperor's New Clothes by Hans Christian Andersen

Goddesses in Everywoman by Jean Shinoda Bolen

Goddesses in Older Women by Jean Shinoda Bolen

Here All Dwell Free by Gertrud Mueller Nelson

Owning your own Shadow: Understanding the Dark Side of the Psyche by Robert A. Johnson

Memories, Dreams and Reflections by C.J. Jung

The Language of Archetypes (Audiobook) by Caroline Myss

Sacred Contracts: Awakening Your Divine Potential by Caroline Myss

Web sites:

crystalinks.com/archetypes.html

splash.net.au/goddess2/goddesssophia/goddess.html

harbour.sfu.ca/~hayward/van/glossary/sophia.html

crystalinks.com/sophia.html

wiu.edu/users/mfjks/303sfa.html

goddessgift.com/goddess-myths/sophia-goddess-wisdom.htm

The Gift of Courage

○ ○

Focus on where you want to go, not on what you fear.

—*Anthony Robbins*

2000

September 23

I have a delightful dream.

Wearing a red, shimmering dress on a stage in a 1920s speakeasy while performing in front of a packed house, I announce I am leaving my old life and starting a new one. Everyone applauds and cheers, and I sing with full bravado. I awaken with a smile on my face, feeling empowered.

A new year arrived, and I had a fresh energy I had never experienced before. I was tired of the leash depression kept me on, tired of being too frightened to experience adventure.

I was reading Phil Cousineau's book, The Art *of Pilgrimage,* at the same time I happened upon an ad in a travel magazine—a trip to discover the ancient myths and sacred sites of Ireland. One of the hosts was none other than Phil Cousineau. It was a serendipitous sign.

My friends and family encouraged me. So, I left in the spring for my first trip abroad.

2001

May 17

Boarding at Denver International Airport, I start my journey into an unknown world. I am filled with excitement and wonder. I am not afraid.

May 18

My first night in Ireland is in Ballyvanugh at the Hyland's Hotel. I am so stimulated I can hardly sleep.

The hand-built stonewalls ramble along the narrow roads. When you meet another vehicle, one of you must pull to the side so the other can pass. The roads are hilly and winding, and multishades of green surround you.

My hair curls as the moist climate infiltrates my body. It is quiet as I sit beside an inlet where an old boat has been abandoned in a marshy swamp. My skin inhales the moisture.

Nearby is a sign that points to a "bird hide." I assume birds nest there. The old village cottages are made from stone, and the roofs and yards are filled with plants. Many of the trees droop and remind me of New Orleans.

May 19

Before we left for the Burren in County Clare, I read the card I purchased in Ballyvanugh: "Come with me oh human child, to the waters and the wild." W.B.Yeats. The words continue to replay themselves.

In the Burren, I sit on a rocky hillside as cattle graze below me. A bird sings, and the wind moves my hair.

Silence appears and smiles at me. Upon the rocks, ivy grows and water glistens upon the ivy leaves; light and dark create the dance of the breeze.

May 21

The Cliffs of Mohr in County Clare touch my soul. In my journey, this is the first place where time and place disappeared. Depression was no longer part of my world; Brainturd didn't exist.

As my head hangs over the cliffs, I listen as the violent ocean crashes against the rocks far below me. I see the seabirds scurry as the waves come in. In my mind, I become part of the sea and know I must fear nothing.

It is here I unwrap the gift of courage. I have traveled to Ireland to both lose and find myself. It is because of the sea that I found myself.

Upon returning to the United States, I realized my journey of ancient myths and sacred sites had opened a door. I was no longer a frightened person afraid of the unknown.

A journey out of the darkness of fear and into the light of self-confidence provided a powerful tool. I left behind the mundane chores and found myself. I discovered things about me that lay hidden. My eyes were opened to new adventures. I discovered it was not weird to want to be alone, to get lost by staring off in space, to enjoy silence, and to like myself.

The concept of the journey struck me so deeply that I created another assemblage.

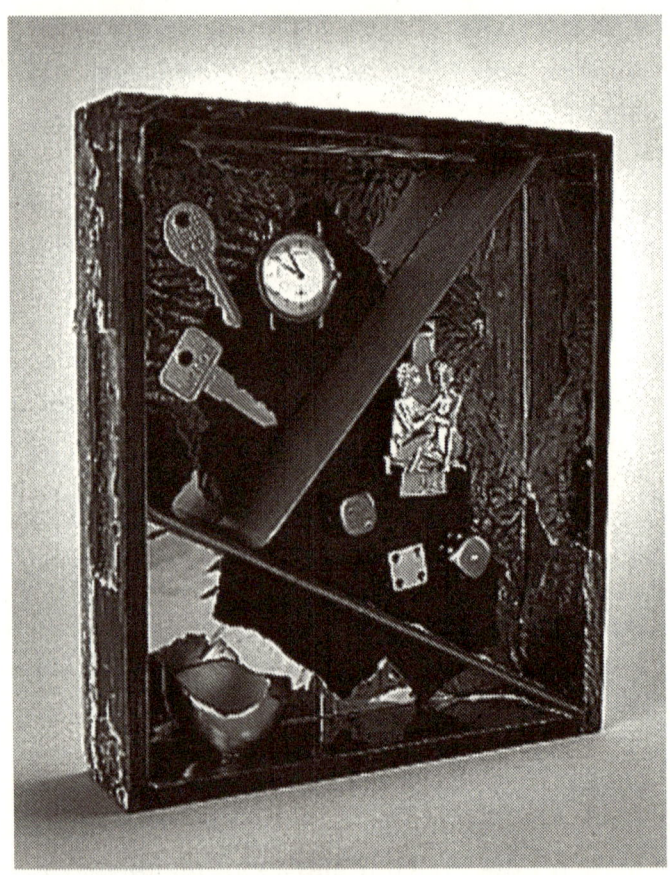

The Journey

"The Journey" contains a key unlocking the entry into the unknown, an open eggshell, a golden image of the twins Gemini, three dice symbolizing the unexpected, and the face of a watch showing our movement. Depression has taught me that courage is much less painful than living in fear. I now know I can travel alone; there is no need to be afraid of what lies before me. I can take care of myself. My depression gave me the gift of courage.

Friend to Friend

Change can be frightening, but life is boring without it. There is a saying by Seung Sahn: "If you don't enter the lion's den, you will never capture the lion." There are those who say that if you don't enter the lion's den, you will not be bitten. For me, the journey of exploration is worth a few bites.

Is fear holding you captive? I hope there will come a time when you are simply tired of feeling afraid, and courage will come to you like the sunrise after a long dark night. Then you will be able to embrace the darkness for what it can teach you. Your self-confidence will grow, and you will not be afraid of what lies ahead.

Creative Healing

Try some of these ideas to explore your fears and invite courage into your life:

• Take a trip by yourself to someplace you have never been. Your travel agent can tell you about inexpensive, all-inclusive trips abroad. Take photos and write in your journal. How is this adventure different from your everyday life? In what ways is your courage rewarded? How can you incorporate what you learn into your life at home?

• Sketch, sculpt, paint, or sew a lion, a long-standing symbol of courage. As you create the parts of the lion's body, think about how the lion displays courage. In what ways can you become more lion-hearted?

• Find an object that represents courage to you—natural wonders like the ocean or a mountain, or perhaps a photo of your grandmother, or a souvenir from a trip you took by yourself. In either poetry or prose, describe the object and how it symbolizes courage.

Helpful Resources

Books:

The Art of Pilgrimage by Phil Cousineau

Snow Leopard by Peter Matthiessen

The Scarlet Letter by Nathaniel Hawthorne

Movies:

Under the Tuscan Sun

Something's Gotta Give

As Good as It Gets

Forrest Gump

Web sites:

en.wikipedia.org/wiki/Castor_and_Polydeuces

paranormal.about.com/library/weekly/aa031102a.htm

authenticireland.com/travel_guide/clare.htm#burren

The Gift of Being True to Myself

No man can wear one face to himself and another to the multitude without finally getting bewildered as to which may be true.

—Nathaniel Hawthorne

1993

February 12

I am doing what my world says I should do, and that sucks. When is it my turn? How old do I have to be before I can live life on my own terms? Our children have left home and are living lives I envy. My husband is a wonderful man who wants me to continue my domestic endeavors; however, I no longer want to be Suzy Homemaker. I want to be an independent woman with my own business.

I've fixed all the hot gruel I ever want to. I have no desire to clean, make the bed, do the laundry, keep the bills paid, buy the groceries, be nice to someone I don't want to spend time with, entertain, or do anything else Beaver Cleaver's mom did. But how I can stop being the person those who love me expect me to be?

When my mom was about to graduate from high school, she wanted to go to college and study art. Her father said she could either be a doctor or an attorney, but he would pay for no other path. Mom's dreams never came true. She never got to know the joy of finding herself; perhaps that is why she drank.

I know how Mom felt. Looking back at my journal entries, I noticed, up until a few years ago, I had suffered the same fate. But look how things have changed since I began unwrapping the gifts depression offered.

2001

September 21

The road I am traveling is taking a turn, and I have walked unknowingly through an unseen opening. The voice inside me says, "Go ahead. Why not? You need to change."

September 28

My husband tells me I dwell in a make-believe land. I tell him it is an enchanting place, and he should try it.

Of all the gifts I have received on this journey, the greatest has been awareness of who I am. I am no longer afraid to stand up for myself. I am often conscious of my thoughts, my actions, and my needs and the needs of others. I have learned that I like warm orange juice, water without ice, daydreaming, silence, reading books, time alone, and taking long walks. I even walk taller.

I'm aware of methods I can use to keep me from reentering depression. I realize when I become tired that I need to relax and take a nap. Before depression, I thought naps were a waste of time; now I know they are as important to me as water without ice.

As for house chores, I've learned there is a big difference in wanting to do something and having to do something. I no longer feel guilty if the ironing piles up and the furniture needs dusting. I play my favorite music when I need to clean or iron, set a time limit—maybe fifteen to thirty minutes—and enjoy myself.

I prioritize what is most important to me, and I have become an independent woman with my own business. I now have my own Web site, create art that is meaningful to me, and enjoy my life.

One day we were visiting friends in Vail, Colorado. The guys were playing golf, and we gals had a "giggle lunch" and chatted our way in and out of shops. One of the stores was filled with imaginative hats, and we delighted in trying them on. The owner was kind enough to take our photograph. What fun it was to let go and be ourselves!

What a change from the way I used to be! I feel as though I have come home. My daughter gave me an old suitcase with her initials on it, and it evolved into my homecoming gift.

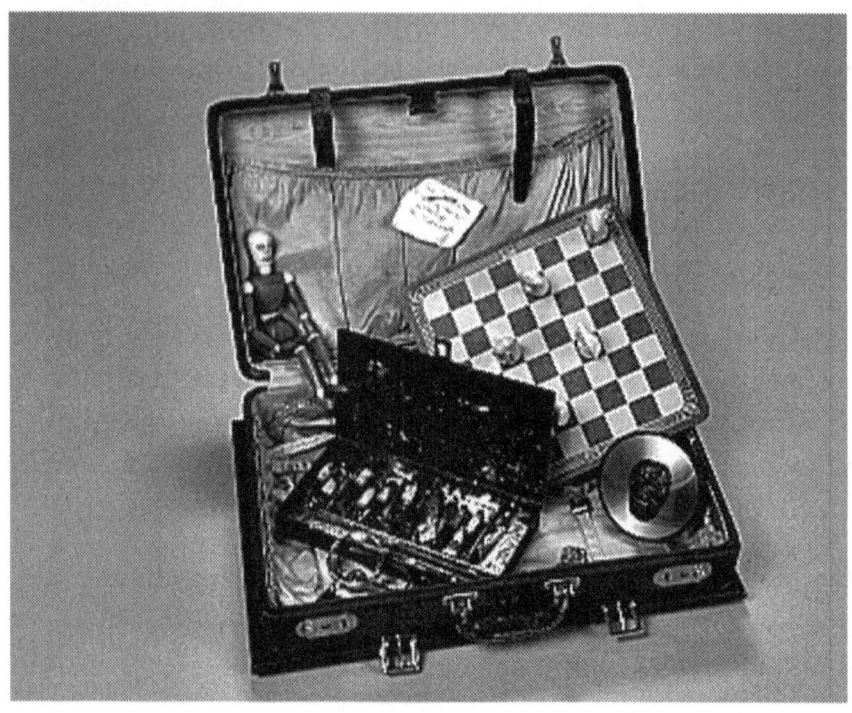

The Way Home

The old, metal box filled with used tubes of oil paint is a symbol for the variety of paths I have taken. Not all of the corridors led in the direction I wanted to go, but I needed to see where they would take me. A mannequin sits in the corner and watches, perhaps aware of what lies ahead. A mask on a round disk leans against a checkered board, as assorted figures contemplate their next move.

The assemblage began with an old suitcase and a handwritten note safety-pinned to its lining. On the note I penned, "Sometimes the only way home is through the basement." I had spent a lot of time in the cellar. I am glad to have climbed the stairs.

Friend to Friend

Your being may be reeling with depression as a warning to wake up and be yourself. Are you denying the authentic you?

Most of us are not what we appear. We try to be who we think others expect us to be, and we hide the genuine person inside. We do not realize we are destroying what we were meant to be.

It is not easy to be yourself. There will be many who are critical of what you do and how you do it. There are those who will have trouble accepting people who are outspoken (no matter how charismatic they themselves are) or those who like to be alone, or those who daydream, keep a journal, or meditate. But we must please ourselves.

On my coffee mug is written, "Dance as though no one is watching, love as though you have never been hurt, sing as though no one can hear you, and live as though heaven is on earth." It reminds me to be true to myself. There is no greater gift.

Creative Healing

Try some of these ideas to discover your true self:

• Keep a journal. At the end of a year, read it from the beginning. How have you changed? In what ways have you become more yourself? What changes can you implement to let more of you into your everyday life?

• Write the following sentence in your journal, continuing with whatever thoughts follow: "If no one were watching, I would _____."

• Make an "All About Me" collage of your favorite things. Go through magazines or catalogs and clip the photos and articles that make you smile. Arrange them on the collage until they feel right, and glue them down. If you can't find or create the images, write them into your art piece.

• Designate an afternoon to sort through your childhood photos, memorabilia, and yearbooks. What did you dream about as a child? What were your talents? What things delighted you?

• Schedule a day once a month to do exactly as you like. Go on a hike, book a raft trip, visit a museum, or stay home and savor a good book. End the day by eating at your favorite restaurant, watching an upbeat movie, or playing your favorite music.

• Go to a ceramic studio and paint mottos or emblems on a coffee mug that rev your engine. After it is glazed, drink your coffee or tea from it, or put it where you will see it daily, and fill it with your pens.

Helpful Resources

Books:

Minding the Body, Mending the Mind by Joan Borysenko

Siddhartha by Hermann Hesse

Gandhi An Autobiography: The Story of My Experiments With Truth by M.K.Gandhi

It's Not About the Bike: My Journey Back to Life by Lance Armstrong, Sally Jenkins

Rosa Parks by Rosa Parks, Jim Haskins

Movies:

Dead Poets Society

Gandhi

Forrest Gump

Web sites:

spiritualcinemacircle.com

trans4mind.com

Boyceco.com [This site is about psychotherapy, personal change, growth, responsibility and hope. Gregory J. Boyce, a personal change therapist, constructed it.]

Postlude: Finding Your Gifts

In the well-known fairy tale, a princess kisses a frog, and the kiss transforms the creature into a prince. The moral of the story? Embrace the ugly and disgusting things in your life, and watch them change into beautiful gifts.

Perhaps now that you have finished my book, you're thinking I had some sort of special power to overcome my depression. If I did, it was only that I was brave enough to embrace my depression and everything that could help me. You can be brave, too. Bravery requires no talent; it's just being so sick and tired of hurting that you're ready to try every avenue of help.

You have gifts waiting for you. How do you get over the hurt and open the gifts?

• See your doctor and get medication. The proper medicines will rebalance your brain chemistry.

• See your counselor for talk therapy. Uncover the hidden sources of pain and heal them.

• Seek the support of others. Your friends and family love you and want to help.

We will have setbacks—on those days, cry, feel sorry for yourself and ask "Why me?" The next day, take another step as you move forward.

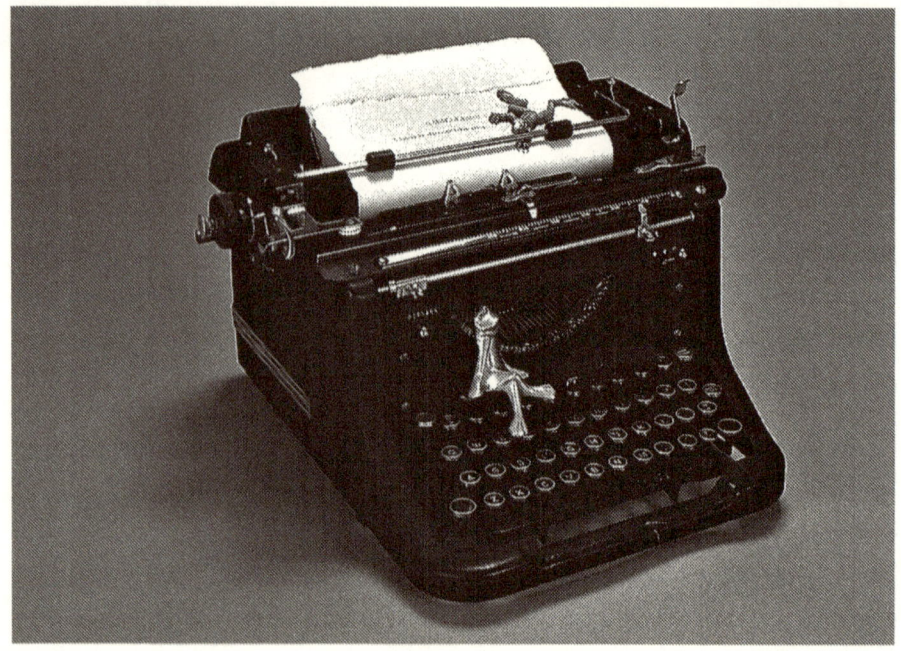

To Kiss a Frog

I wish you the courage to kiss your frog.

Index

978-0-595-42527-3
0-595-42527-5